Presented to

....

From

....

On this Date

....

a collection of

Love gifts

HELEN STEINER RICE

A DAYMAKER GREETING BOOK

the magic of love

Love is like *magic* and it always will be,
   for love still remains *life's sweet mystery!*
Love works in ways that are wondrous and strange
   and there's *nothing in life* that *love cannot change!*
Love can transform the most commonplace
   into beauty and splendor and sweetness and grace!
Love is unselfish, understanding and kind,
   for it sees with its *heart* and not with its mind!
Love is the answer that everyone seeks—
Love is the language that every heart speaks—
Love can't be bought, it is priceless and free,
Love like pure *magic* is a *sweet mystery!*

THERE'S SUNSHINE IN A SMILE

Life is a mixture of
sunshine and rain,
Laughter and pleasure,
teardrops and pain,
All days can't be bright,
but it's certainly true,
There was never a cloud
    the sun didn't shine through—
So just keep on smiling
whatever betide you,
Secure in the knowledge
    God is always beside you,

And you'll find when you smile
    your day will be brighter
And all of your burdens
    will seem so much lighter—
For each time you smile
you will find it is true
Somebody, somewhere
will *smile back at you,*
And nothing on earth
    can make life
more worthwhile
Than the sunshine and warmth
of a *beautiful smile.*

THE POWER OF LOVE

There is no thinking person
    who can stand untouched today
And view the world around us
    drifting downward to decay
Without feeling deep within them
    a silent unnamed dread,
Wondering how to stem the chaos
    that lies frightfully ahead. . .
But the problems we are facing
    cannot humanly be solved
For our diplomatic strategy
    only gets us more involved
And our skillful ingenuity,
    our technology and science
Can never change a sinful heart
    filled with hatred and defiance. . .
So our problems keep on growing
    every hour of every day
As man vainly tries to solve them
    in his own *self-willful way*. . .
But man is powerless alone
    to clean up the world outside
Until his own polluted soul
    is *clean and free inside*. . .
For the amazing power of love
    is beyond all comprehension
And it alone can heal this world
    of its hatred and dissension.

WARM OUR HEARTS WITH THY LOVE

Oh, God, who made the summer
    and warmed the earth with beauty,
Warm our hearts with gratitude
    and devotion to our duty,
For in this age of violence,
    rebellion and defiance
We've forgotten the true meaning
    of "dependable reliance"—
We have lost our sense of duty
    and our sense of values, too,
And what was once unsanctioned,
    no longer is taboo,
Our standards have been lowered
    and we resist all discipline,
And our vision has been narrowed
    and blinded to all sin—
Oh, put the summer brightness
    in our closed, unseeing eyes
So in the careworn faces
    that we pass we'll recognize
The heartbreak and the loneliness,
    the trouble and despair
That a word of understanding
    would make easier to bear—
Oh, God, look down on our cold hearts
    and warm them with Your love,
And grant us Your forgiveness
    which we're so unworthy of.

Count your gains and not your losses.

my garden of prayer

My garden beautifies my yard

and adds fragrance to the air. . .

But it is also my cathedral

and my quiet place of prayer. . .

So little do we realize

that "the glory and the power"

Of He who made the universe

lies hidden in a flower.

COUNT YOUR GAINS
AND NOT YOUR LOSSES

As we travel down life's busy road
  complaining of our heavy load,
We often think God's been unfair
  and gave us much more than our share
Of little daily irritations
  and disappointing tribulations. . .
We're discontented with our lot
  and all the "bad breaks" that we got,
We count our losses, not our gain,
  and remember only tears and pain. . .
The good things we forget completely
  when God looked down
  and blessed us sweetly,
Our troubles fill our every thought,
  we dwell upon lost goals we sought,
And wrapped up in our own despair
  we have no time to see or share
Another's load that far outweighs
  our little problems and dismays. . .
And so we walk with head held low
  and little do we guess or know
That someone near us on life's street
  is burdened deeply with defeat. . .
But if we'd but forget *our care*
  and stop in sympathy to share
The burden that "our brother" carried,
  our mind and heart
  would be less harried
And we would feel our load was small,
  in fact, *we carried no load at all.*

THE PEACE OF MEDITATION

So we may know God better
And feel His quiet power,
Let us daily keep in silence
A *meditation hour*—
For to understand God's greatness
And to use His gifts each day
The soul must learn to meet Him
In a meditative way,
For our Father tells His children
That if they would know His will
They must seek Him in the silence
When all is calm and still. . .
For nature's greatest forces
Are found in quiet things
Like softly falling snowflakes
Drifting down on angels' wings,
Or petals dropping soundlessly
From a lovely full-blown rose,
So God comes closest to us
When our souls are in repose. . .
So let us plan with prayerful care
To always allocate
A certain portion of each day
To be still and meditate. . .
For when everything is quiet
And we're lost in meditation,
Our soul is then preparing
For a deeper dedication
That will make it wholly possible
To quietly endure
The violent world around us—
For in God we are secure.

IF YOU MEET GOD
IN THE MORNING,
HE'LL GO WITH YOU
THROUGH THE DAY
"The earth is the Lord's
    and the fulness thereof"—
It speaks of His greatness,
    it sings of His love,
And each day at dawning
    I lift my heart high
And raise up my eyes
    to the infinite sky. . .
I watch the night vanish
    as a new day is born,

And I hear the birds sing
    on the wings of the morn,
I see the dew glisten
    in crystal-like splendor
While God, with a touch
    that is gentle and tender,
Wraps up the night
    and softly tucks it away
And hangs out the sun
    to herald a new day. . .
And so I give thanks
    and my heart kneels to pray—
"God, keep me and guide me
    and go with me today."

13

finding faith in a flower

Sometimes when faith is running low
And I cannot fathom *why things are so. . .*
I walk alone among the flowers I grow
And learn the *"answers"* to *all I would know!*
For among my flowers I have come to see
Life's *miracle* and its *mystery. . .*
And standing in silence and reverie
My *faith comes flooding back to me!*

IT'S A WONDERFUL WORLD

In spite of the fact
    we complain and lament
And view this old world
    with much discontent,
Deploring conditions
    and grumbling because
There's so much injustice
    and so many flaws,
It's a wonderful world
    and it's people like you
Who make it that way
    by the things that they do—
For a warm, ready smile
    or a kind, thoughtful deed,
Or a hand outstretched
    in an hour of need
Can change our whole outlook
    and make the world bright
Where a minute before
    just nothing seemed right—
It's a *wonderful world*
    and it always will be
If we keep our eyes open
    and focused to see
The *wonderful things*
    man is capable of
When he opens his heart
    to *God* and *His love.*

BE OF GOOD CHEER— THERE'S NOTHING TO FEAR!

Cheerful thoughts like sunbeams
Lighten up the "darkest fears"
For when the heart is happy
There's just no time for tears—
And when the face is smiling
It's impossible to frown,
And when you are "high-spirited"
You cannot feel "low-down"—
For the nature of our attitude
Toward circumstantial things
Determines our acceptance
Of the problems that life brings,

And since fear and dread and worry
Cannot help in any way,
It's much healthier and happier
To be cheerful every day—
And if you'll only try it
You will find, without a doubt,
A cheerful attitude's something
No one should be without—
For when the heart is cheerful
It cannot be filled with fear,
And without fear the way ahead
Seems more distinct and clear—
And we realize there's nothing
We need ever face alone
For our Heavenly Father loves us
and our problems are His own.

HE LOVES YOU!
It's amazing and incredible,
But it's as true as it can be,
God loves and understands us all
And that means *you* and *me*—
His grace is all sufficient
For both the *young* and *old*,
For the lonely and the timid,
For the brash and for the bold—
His love knows no exceptions,
So never feel excluded
No matter *who* or *what* you are
Your name has been included—
And no matter what your past has been,

Trust God to understand,
And no matter what your problem is
Just place it in His Hand—
For in all of our *unloveliness*
This *great God loves us still,*
He loved us since the world began
And what's more, *He always will!*

WHAT MORE CAN YOU ASK
God's love endureth forever—
What a wonderful thing to know
When the tides of life run against you
And your spirit is downcast and low. . .
God's kindness is ever around you,
Always ready to freely impart
Strength to your faltering spirit,
Cheer to your lonely heart. . .
God's presence is ever beside you,
As near as the reach of your hand,
You have but to tell Him your troubles,
There is nothing He won't understand. . .
And knowing God's love is unfailing,
And His mercy unending and great,
You have but to trust in His promise—
"God comes not too soon or too late". . .
So wait with a heart that is patient
For the goodness of God to prevail—
For never do prayers go unanswered,
And His mercy and love never fail.

let go and let God!

When you're troubled and worried and sick at heart

And your plans are upset and your world falls apart,

Remember God's ready and waiting to share

The burden you find much too heavy to bear —

So with faith, "let go" and "let God" lead the way

Into a brighter and less troubled day.

"FLOWERS LEAVE THEIR
FRAGRANCE ON THE HAND
THAT BESTOWS THEM"
There's an old Chinese proverb
    that, if practiced each day,
Would change the whole world
    in a wonderful way—
Its truth is so simple,
    it's so easy to do,
And it works every time
    and successfully, too. . .

For you can't do a kindness
    without a reward,
Not in silver nor gold
    but in joy from the Lord—
You can't light a candle
    to show others the way
Without feeling the warmth
    of that bright little ray. . .
And you can't pluck a rose,
    all fragrant with dew,
Without part of its fragrance
    remaining with you.

LOOK ON THE SUNNY SIDE
There are always two sides,
    the *good* and the *bad*,
The *dark* and the *light*,
    the *sad* and the *glad*—
But in looking back over
    the *good* and the *bad*
We're aware of the number
    of *good things* we've had—
And in counting our blessings
    we find when we're through
We've no reason at all
    to complain or be blue—
So thank God for *good* things
    He has already done,
And be grateful to Him
    for the battles you've won,
And know that the same God
    who helped you before
Is ready and willing
    to help you once more—
Then with faith in your heart
    reach out for God's Hand
And accept what He sends,
    though you can't understand—
For *Our Father* in heaven
    always knows what is best,
And if you trust in His wisdom
    your life will be blest,
For always remember
    that whatever betide you,

You are never alone
    for God is beside you.

TODAY'S JOY WAS BORN
OF YESTERDAY'S SORROW
Who said the "darkness of the
night" would never turn to day,
Who said the "winter's bleakness"
would never pass away,
Who said the fog would never lift
and let the sunshine through,
Who said the skies now overcast
would nevermore be blue—
Why should we ever entertain
these thoughts so dark and grim
And let the brightness of our mind
grow cynical and dim
When we know beyond
all questioning
that winter turns to spring
And on the notes of sorrow
new songs are made to sing—
For no one sheds a teardrop
or suffers loss in vain,
For God is always there to turn
our losses into gain,
And every burden born today
and every present sorrow
Are but God's happy harbingers
of a joyous, bright tomorrow.

God
is never
beyond our
reach.

"ON THE WINGS OF PRAYER"

Just close your eyes
    and open your heart
And feel your worries
    and cares depart,
Just yield yourself
    to the Father above
And let Him hold you
    secure in His love—
For life on earth
    grows more involved
With endless problems
    that can't be solved—
But God only asks us
    to do our best,
Then He will "take over"
    and finish the rest—
So when you are tired,
    discouraged and blue,
There's always one door
    that is open to you—
And that is the door
    to "The House of Prayer"
And you'll find God waiting
    to meet you there,
And "The House of Prayer"
    is no farther away
Than the quiet spot
    where you kneel and pray—
For the heart is a temple
    when God is there

As we place ourselves
    in His loving care,
And He hears every prayer
    and answers each one
When we pray in His name
    "Thy will be done"—
And the burdens that seemed
    too heavy to bear
Are lifted away
    on *"the wings of prayer."*

BRIGHTEN THE CORNER
WHERE YOU ARE

We cannot all be famous
or be listed in *"Who's Who,"*
But every person great or small
has important work to do,
For seldom do we realize
the importance of small deeds
Or to what degree of greatness
unnoticed kindness leads—
For it's not the big celebrity
in a world of fame and praise,
But it's doing unpretentiously
in undistinguished ways
The work that God assigned to us,
unimportant as it seems,
That makes our task outstanding
and brings reality to dreams—
So do not sit and idly wish
for wider, new dimensions
Where you can put in practice
your many *"good intentions"*—
But at the spot God placed you
begin at once to do
Little things to brighten up
the lives surrounding you,
For if everybody brightened up
the spot on which
they're standing
By being more considerate
and a little less demanding,

This dark old world would very soon
eclipse the "Evening Star"
If everybody *brightened up*
the corner where they are!

SOMEONE CARES

Someone cares and always will,
The world forgets
but God loves you still,
You cannot go beyond His Love
No matter what you're guilty of—
For God forgives until the end,
He is your faithful, loyal friend,
And though you try to hide your face
There is no shelter any place
That can escape His watchful eye,
For on the earth and in the sky
He's ever present and *always there*
To take you in His tender care
And bind the wounds
and mend the breaks
When all the world around forsakes. . .
Someone cares and *loves you still*
And *God* is *the Someone*
who always will.

it takes the bitter and the sweet to make a life full and complete

Life is a mixture of sunshine and rain,
Laughter and teardrops, pleasure and pain—
Low tides and high tides, mountains and plains,
Triumphs, defeats and losses and gains—
But *always* in *all ways* God's guiding and leading
And He alone knows the things we're most needing—
And when He sends sorrow or some dreaded affliction,
Be assured that it comes with God's kind benediction—
And if we accept it as a *gift of His love*,
We'll be showered with blessings from *Our Father above.*

WHEN TROUBLES ASSAIL YOU, GOD WILL NOT FAIL YOU

When life seems empty
And there's no place to go,
When your heart is troubled
And your spirits are low,
When friends seem few
And nobody cares
There is always God
To hear your prayers—
And whatever you're facing
Will seem much less
When you go to God
And confide and confess,
For the burden that seems
Too heavy to bear
God lifts away
On the wings of prayer—
And seen through God's eyes
Earthly troubles diminish
And we're given new strength
To face and to finish
Life's daily tasks
As they come along
If we pray for strength
To keep us strong—
So go to Our Father
When troubles assail you
For His grace is sufficient
And He'll never fail you.

GREAT FAITH THAT SMILES IS BORN OF GREAT TRIALS

It's easy to say *"In God we trust"*
When life is radiant and fair,
But the test of faith is only found
When there are burdens to bear—
For our claim to faith
in the "sunshine"
Is really *no faith at all*,
For when roads are smooth
and days are bright
Our need for God is so small,
And no one discovers the fullness
Or the greatness of God's love
Unless they have walked
in the "darkness"
With only a *light* from *above*—
For the faith to endure
whatever comes
Is born of sorrow and trials,
And strengthened only by discipline
And nurtured by self-denials—
So be not disheartened by troubles,
For trials are the "building blocks"
On which to erect a *fortress* of *faith*
Secure on God's "ageless rocks."

DAILY PRAYERS
DISSOLVE YOUR CARES

I meet God in the morning
And go with Him through the day,
Then in the stillness of the night
Before sleep comes I pray
That God will just "take over"
All the problems I couldn't solve
And in the peacefulness of sleep
My cares will all dissolve,
So when I open up my eyes
To greet another day
I'll find myself renewed in strength
And there'll open up a way
To meet what seemed impossible
For me to solve alone
And once again I'll be assured
I am never *"on my own"*. . .
For if we try to stand alone
We are weak and we will fall,
For God is always *Greatest*
When we're helpless, lost and small,
And no day is unmeetable
If on rising our first thought
Is to thank God for the blessings
That His loving care has brought. . .
For there can be no failures
Or hopeless, unsaved sinners
If we enlist the help of God
Who makes all losers winners. . .

So meet Him in the morning
And go with Him through the day
And thank Him for His guidance
Each evening when you pray,
And if you follow faithfully
This daily way to pray
You will never in your lifetime
Face another "hopeless day."

HELP YOURSELF TO HAPPINESS

Everybody, everywhere
    seeks happiness, it's true,
But finding it and keeping it
    seems difficult to do,
Difficult because we think
    that happiness is found
Only in the places where
    wealth and fame abound—
And so we go on searching
    in "palaces of pleasure"
Seeking recognition
    and monetary treasure,
Unaware that happiness
    is just a "state of mind"
Within the reach of everyone
    who takes time to be kind—
For in making *others happy*
    we will be happy, too,
For the happiness you give away
    returns to "shine on you."

BLESSINGS IN DISGUISE
ARE DIFFICULT TO RECOGNIZE

God sends His "little angels"
in many forms and guises,
They come as lovely miracles
that God alone devises—
For He does nothing
without purpose,
everything's a perfect plan
To fulfill in bounteous measure
all He ever promised man—
For every "little angel"
with a body bent and broken,
Or a little mind retarded
or little words unspoken,
Is just God's way of trying
to reach and touch the hand
Of all who do not know Him
and cannot understand
That often through an angel
whose "wings will never fly"
The Lord is pointing out the way
to His eternal sky
Where there will be no handicaps
of body, soul or mind,
And where all limitations
will be dropped and left behind—
So accept these "little angels"
as gifts from God above
And thank Him for this lesson
in Faith and Hope and Love.

GOOD MORNING, GOD!

You are ushering in another day
Untouched and freshly new
So here I come to ask You, God,
If You'll renew me, too,
Forgive the many errors
That I made yesterday
And let me try again, dear God,
To walk closer in Thy way. . .
But, Father, I am well aware
I can't make it on my own
So take my hand and hold it tight
For I can't walk alone!

A THANKFUL HEART

Take nothing for granted,
for whenever you do
The "joy of enjoying"
is lessened for you—
For we rob our own lives
much more than we know
When we fail to respond
or in any way show
Our thanks for the blessings
that daily are ours. . .
The warmth of the sun,
the fragrance of flowers,
The beauty of twilight,
the freshness of dawn,
The coolness of dew
on a green velvet lawn,
The kind little deeds
so thoughtfully done,
The favors of friends
and the love that someone
Unselfishly gives us
in a myriad of ways,
Expecting no payment
and no words of praise—
Oh, great is our loss
when we no longer find
A thankful response
to things of this kind,
For the joy of enjoying
and the Fullness of living
Are found in the heart
that is filled with
Thanksgiving.

thank God for little things

Thank You, God, for little things
    that often come our way—
The things we take for granted
    but don't mention when we pray—
The unexpected courtesy,
    the thoughtful, kindly deed—
A hand reached out to help us
    in the time of sudden need—
Oh make us more aware, dear God,
    of little daily graces
That come to us with "sweet surprise"
    from never-dreamed-of places.

TROUBLE IS A STEPPING-STONE TO GROWTH

Trouble is something
no one can escape,
Everyone has it in
some form or shape—
Some people hide it
way down deep inside,
Some people bear it
with gallant-like pride,
Some people worry
and complain of their lot,
Some people covet
what they haven't got,
While others rebel and
become bitter and old
With hopes that are dead
and hearts that are cold. . .
But the wise man accepts
whatever God sends,
Willing to yield like
a storm-tossed tree bends,
Knowing that God never
makes a mistake,
So whatever He sends
they are willing to take—
For trouble is part
and parcel of life
And no man can grow
without trouble and strife,
And the steep hills ahead
and high mountain peaks
Afford man at last
the peace that he seeks—
So blest are the people
who learn to accept
The trouble men try
to escape and reject,
For in our acceptance
we're given great grace
And courage and faith
and the strength to face
The daily troubles
that come to us all
So we may learn to stand
"straight and tall"—
For the grandeur of life
is born of defeat
For in overcoming
we make life complete.

a favorite recipe

Take a cup of kindness,

mix it well with love,

Add a lot of Patience

and faith in God above,

Sprinkle very generously

with joy and thanks and cheer —

And you'll have lots of "angel food"

to feast on all the year.

THE MYSTERY OF PRAYER

Beyond that which
words can interpret
Or theology can explain
The soul feels
a "shower of refreshment"
That falls like the gentle rain
On hearts that are
parched with problems
And are searching to find the way
To somehow attract God's attention
Through well-chosen words
as they pray,

Not knowing that God
in His wisdom
Can sense all man's worry and woe
For there is nothing man can conceal
That God does not already know. . .
So kneel in prayer in His presence
And you'll find no need to speak
For softly in silent communion
God grants you
the peace that you seek.

FATHERS ARE WONDERFUL PEOPLE

Fathers are wonderful people
    too little understood,
And we do not sing their praises
    as often as we should. . .
For, somehow, Father seems to be
    the man who pays the bills,
While Mother binds up little hurts
    and nurses all our ills. . .
And Father struggles daily
    to live up to *"his image"*
As protector and provider
    and "hero of the scrimmage". . .
And perhaps that is the reason
    we sometimes get the notion
That Fathers are not subject
    to the thing we call emotion,
But if you look inside Dad's heart,
    where no one else can see,
You'll find he's sentimental
    and as "soft" as he can be. . .
But he's so busy every day
    in the grueling race of life,
He leaves the sentimental stuff
    to his partner and his wife. . .
But Fathers are just *wonderful*
    in a million different ways,
And they merit loving compliments
    and accolades of praise,
For the only reason Dad aspires
    to fortune and success
Is to make the family proud of him
    and to bring them happiness. . .
And like *Our Heavenly Father*,
    he's a guardian and a guide,
Someone that we can count on
    to be *always on our side.*

AFTER THE WINTER. . . GOD SENDS THE SPRING

Springtime is a season
Of Hope and Joy and Cheer,
There's beauty all around us
To see and touch and hear. . .
So, no matter how downhearted
And discouraged we may be,
New Hope is born when we behold
Leaves budding on a tree. . .
Or when we see a timid flower
Push through the frozen sod
And open wide in glad surprise
Its petaled eyes to God. . .
For this is just God saying—
"Lift up your eyes to Me,
And the bleakness of your spirit,
Like the budding springtime tree,
Will lose its wintry darkness
And your heavy heart will sing"—
For God never sends The Winter
Without the Joy of Spring.

"THIS TOO WILL PASS AWAY"

If I can endure for this minute
Whatever is happening to me,
No matter how heavy my heart is
Or how "dark" the moment may be—
If I can remain calm and quiet
With all my world crashing about me,
Secure in the knowledge
God loves me
When everyone else
seems to doubt me—
If I can but keep on believing
What I know in my heart to be true,
That "darkness will fade
with the morning"
And that this will pass away, too—
Then nothing in life can defeat me
For as long as this knowledge remains
I can suffer whatever is happening
For I know God will break
"all the chains"
That are binding me tight
in "the Darkness"
And trying to fill me with fear—
For there is no night
without dawning
And I know that
"my morning" is near.

HE ASKS SO LITTLE
AND GIVES SO MUCH

What must I do
    to insure peace of mind?
Is the answer I'm seeking
    too hard to find?
How can I know
    what God wants me to be?
How can I tell
    what's expected of me?
Where can I go
    for guidance and aid
To help me correct
    the errors I've made?
The answer is found
    in doing *three things*
And great is the gladness
    that doing them brings. . .
"Do justice"—*"Love kindness"*—
    "Walk humbly with God"—
For with these *three things*
    as your "rule and your rod"
All things worth having
    are yours to achieve
If you follow God's words
    and have *faith to believe!*

THANK YOU, GOD,
FOR EVERYTHING

Thank You, God, for everything—
    the big things and the small,
For "every good gift comes from God"—
    the giver of them all—
And all too often we accept
    without any thanks or praise
The gifts God sends as blessings
    each day in many ways,
And so at this *Thanksgiving time*
    we offer up a prayer
To thank You, God, for giving us
    a lot more than our share. . .
First, thank You for the little things
    that often come our way,
The things we take for granted
    but don't mention when we pray,
The unexpected courtesy,
    the thoughtful, kindly deed,
A hand reached out to help us
    in the time of sudden need. . .
Oh, make us more aware, dear God,
    of little daily graces
That come to us with "sweet surprise"
    from never-dreamed-of places—
Then, thank You for the *"Miracles"*
    we are much too blind to see,
And give us new awareness
    of our many gifts from Thee,

And help us to remember
    that the *Key* to *Life* and *Living*
Is to make each prayer
a *Prayer of Thanks*
    and every day *Thanksgiving.*

A SURE WAY TO A HAPPY DAY

Happiness is something
    we create in our mind,
It's not something you search for
    and so seldom find—
It's just waking up
    and beginning the day
By counting our blessings
    and kneeling to pray—
It's giving up thoughts
    that breed discontent
And accepting what comes
    as a "gift heaven-sent"—
It's giving up wishing
    for things we have not
And making the best of
    whatever we've got—
It's knowing that life
    is determined for us,
And pursuing our tasks
    without fret, fume or fuss—
For it's by completing
    what God gives us to do
That we find real contentment
    and happiness, too.

Never
borrow
sorrow from
tomorrow.

EVERYONE NEEDS SOMEONE

People need people
and friends need friends,
And we all need love
for a full life depends
Not on vast riches or great acclaim,
Not on success or on worldly fame,
But just in knowing that
someone cares
And holds us close
in their thoughts and prayers—
For only the knowledge
that we're understood
Makes everyday living
feel wonderfully good,
And we rob ourselves
of life's greatest need
When we "lock up our hearts"
and fail to heed
The outstretched hand
reaching to find
A kindred spirit
whose heart and mind
Are lonely and longing
to somehow share
Our joys and sorrows
and to make us aware
That life's completeness
and richness depends
On the things we share
with our loved ones and friends.

WE CAN'T. . .BUT GOD CAN!

Why things happen as they do
We do not always know,
And we cannot always fathom
Why our spirits sink so low. . .
We flounder in our dark distress,
We are wavering and unstable,
But when we're most inadequate
The Lord God's always able. . .
For though we are incapable,
God's powerful and great,
And there's no darkness of the mind
That God can't penetrate. . .
And all that is required of us
Whenever things go wrong
Is to trust in God implicitly
With a faith that's deep
and strong, And while He may
not instantly Unravel
all the strands Of the tangled
thoughts that trouble us—
He completely understands. . .
And in His time, if we have faith,
He will gradually restore
The brightness to our spirit
That we've been longing for. . .
So remember, there's
    no cloud too dark
For God's light to penetrate
If we keep on believing
And have faith enough to wait!

YESTERDAY. . . TODAY. . . AND TOMORROW!

Yesterday's dead,
Tomorrow's unborn,
So there's nothing to fear
And nothing to mourn,
For all that is past
And all that has been
Can never return
To be lived once again—
And what lies ahead
Or the things that will be
Are still in God's Hands
So it is not up to me
To live in the future
That is God's great unknown,
For the past and the present
God claims for His own,
So all I need do
Is to live for Today
And trust God to show me
The Truth and The Way—
For it's only the memory
Of things that have been
And expecting Tomorrow
To bring trouble again
That fills my Today,
Which God wants to bless,
With uncertain fears
And borrowed distress—
For all I need live for
Is this one little minute,
For life's Here and Now
And Eternity's in it.

"THE HEAVENS DECLARE THE GLORY OF GOD"

You ask me how I know it's true
that here is a living God—
A God who rules the universe,
the sky. . .the sea. . .the sod;
A God who holds all creatures
in the hollow of His hand;
A God who put Infinity
in one tiny grain of sand;
A God who made the seasons—
Winter, Summer, Fall and Spring,
And put His flawless rhythm
into each created thing;
A God who hangs the sun out
slowly with the break of day,
And gently takes the stars in
and puts the night away;
A God whose mighty handiwork
defies the skill of man,
For no architect can alter
God's perfect master plan—
What better answers are there
to prove His Holy Being
Than the wonders all around us
that are ours just for the seeing.

THE WAY TO GOD

If my days were untroubled
and my heart always light
Would I seek that fair land
where there is no night;
If I never grew weary
with the weight of my load
Would I search for God's Peace
at the end of the road;
If I never knew sickness
and never felt pain
Would I reach for a hand
to help and sustain;
If I walked not with sorrow
and lived without loss
Would my soul seek sweet solace
at the foot of the cross;
If all I desired
was mine day by day
Would I kneel before God
and earnestly pray;
If God sent no "Winter"
to freeze me with fear
Would I yearn for the warmth
of "Spring" every year;
I ask myself this
and the answer is plain—
If my life were all pleasure
and I never knew pain
I'd seek God less often
and need Him much less,

For God's sought more often
in times of distress,
And no one knows God
or sees Him as plain
As those who have met Him
on "The Pathway of Pain."

ANYWHERE IS A PLACE
OF PRAYER IF GOD IS THERE
I have prayed on my knees
    in the morning,
I have prayed as I walked along,
I have prayed in the silence
    and darkness
And I've prayed to the tune
    of a song—
I have prayed in the midst
    of triumph
And I've prayed when I
    suffered defeat,
I have prayed on the sands
    of the seashore
Where the waves of the ocean beat—
I have prayed in a velvet-hushed
    forest
Where the quietness calmed my fears,
I have prayed through suffering
    and heartache
When my eyes were blinded
    with tears—
I have prayed in churches
    and chapels,
Cathedrals and synagogues, too,
But often I've had the feeling
That my prayers were
    not getting through,
And I realized then that Our Father

Is not really concerned
    where we pray
Or impressed by our manner of worship
Or the eloquent words that we say. . .
He is only concerned with our feelings,
And He looks deep into our heart
And hears the "cry
    of our soul's deep need"
That no words could ever impart. . .
So it isn't the prayer that's expressive
Or offered in some special spot,
It's the sincere plea of a sinner
And God can tell whether or not
We honestly seek His forgiveness
And earnestly mean what we say,
And then and then only He answers
The prayer that we fervently pray.

THINGS TO BE THANKFUL FOR
The good, green earth beneath our feet,
The air we breathe, the food we eat,
Some work to do, a goal to win,
A hidden longing deep within
That spurs us on to bigger things
And helps us meet what each day brings,
All these things and many more
Are things we should be thankful for. . .
And most of all our thankful prayers
Should rise to God because He cares!

let not your heart
be troubled

Whenever I am troubled and lost in deep despair

I bundle all my troubles up and go to God in prayer. . .

I tell Him I am heartsick and lost and lonely, too,

That my mind is deeply burdened and I don't know what to do. . .

But I know He stilled the tempest and calmed the angry sea

And I humbly ask if in His love He'll do the same for me. . .

And then I just keep quiet and think only thoughts of peace

And if I abide in stillness my "restless murmurings" cease.

THE END OF THE ROAD
IS BUT A BEND IN THE ROAD
When we feel we have nothing
left to give and we are sure
that the "song has ended"—
When our day seems over
and the shadows fall
and the darkness of night
has descended,
Where can we go to find
the strength to valiantly
keep on trying,

Where can we find
the hand that will dry
the tears that the heart is crying—
There's but one place to go
and that is to God
and, dropping all pretense
    and pride,
We can pour out our problems
without restraint
and gain strength
with Him at our side—
And together we stand
at life's crossroads and view
what we think is the end,
But God has a much bigger vision
and He tells us it's only a bend—
For the road goes on
and is smoother,
and the "pause in the song"
is a "rest,"
And the part that's unsung
and unfinished is the sweetest
and richest and best—
So rest and relax
and grow stronger,
Let go and let God
share your load,
Your work is not finished
or ended, you've just come
to "a bend in the road."

give lavishly!
give abundantly!

The more you give, the more you get—
The more you laugh, the less you fret—
The more you do *unselfishly*,
The more you live *abundantly*. . .

The more of everything you share,
The more you'll always have to spare—
The more you love, the more you'll find
That life is good and friends are kind. . .

For only *what we give away*,
Enriches us from day to day.

OPEN MY EYES

God open my eyes
    so I may see
And feel Your presence
    close to me. . .
Give me strength
    for my stumbling feet
As I battle the crowd
    on life's busy street,
And widen the vision
    of my unseeing eyes
So in passing faces
    I'll recognize
Not just a stranger,
    unloved and unknown,
But a friend with a heart
    that is much like my own. . .
Give me perception
    to make me aware
That scattered profusely
    on life's thoroughfare
Are the best *gifts* of *God*
    that we daily pass by
As we look at the world
    with an *unseeing eye.*

NEVER BORROW SORROW
FROM TOMORROW

Deal only with the present,
Never step into tomorrow,
For God asks us just to trust Him
And to never borrow sorrow—
For the future is not ours to know
And it may never be,
So let us live and give our best
And give it lavishly—
For to meet tomorrow's troubles
Before they are even ours
Is to anticipate the Saviour
And to doubt His all-wise powers—
So let us be content to solve
Our problems one by one,
Asking nothing of tomorrow
Except *"Thy will be done."*

GOD KNOWS BEST

Our Father knows
what's best for us,
So why should we complain—
We always want the sunshine,
But He knows there must be rain—
We love the sound of laughter
And the merriment of cheer,
But our hearts would lose
their tenderness
If we never shed a tear. . .
Our Father tests us often
With suffering and with sorrow,
He tests us, not to punish us,
But to help us meet tomorrow. . .
For growing trees are strengthened
When they withstand the storm,
And the sharp cut of the chisel
Gives the marble grace and form. . .
God never hurts us needlessly,
And He never wastes our pain,
For every loss He sends to us
Is followed by rich gain. . .
And when we count the blessings
That God has so freely sent,
We will find no cause for murmuring
And no time to lament. . .
For Our Father loves His children,
And to Him all things are plain,
So He never sends us pleasure
When the soul's deep need is pain. . .
So whenever we are troubled,
And when everything goes wrong,
It is just God working in us
To make our spirit strong.

THE GOLDEN CHAIN
OF FRIENDSHIP

Friendship is a golden chain,
The links are friends so dear,
And like a rare and precious jewel
It's treasured more each year. . .
It's clasped together firmly
With a love that's deep and true,
And it's rich with happy memories
And fond recollections, too. . .
Time can't destroy its beauty
For, as long as memory lives,
Years can't erase the pleasure
That the joy of friendship gives. . .
For friendship is a priceless gift
That can't be bought or sold,
But to have an understanding friend
Is worth far more than gold. . .
And the golden chain or friendship
Is a strong and blessed tie
Binding kindred hearts together
As the years go passing by.

blessings
in disguise
are difficult
to recognize.

how great the yield
from a fertile field

The farmer ploughs through the fields of green
And the blade of the plough is sharp and keen,
But the seed must be sown to bring forth grain,
For nothing is born without suffering and pain—
And God never ploughs in the soul of man
Without intention and purpose and plan,
So whenever you feel the plough's sharp blade
Let not your heart be sorely afraid
For, like the farmer, God chooses a field
From which He expects an excellent yield—
So rejoice though your heart is broken in two,
God seeks to bring forth a rich harvest in you.

WHEN TROUBLE COMES
AND THINGS GO WRONG!

Let us go quietly to God
when troubles come to us,
Let us never stop to whimper
or complain and fret and fuss,
Let us hide "our thorns" in "roses"
and our sighs in "golden song"
And "our crosses"
in a "crown of smiles"
whenever things go wrong. . .
For no one can really help us
as our troubles we bemoan,
For comfort, help and inner peace
must come from God alone. . .
So do not tell your neighbor,
your companion or your friend
In the hope that they can help you
bring your troubles to an end. . .
For they, too, have their problems,
they are burdened just like you,
So take your cross to Jesus
and He will see you through. . .
And waste no time in crying
on the shoulder of a friend
But go directly to the Lord
for on Him you can depend. . .
For there's absolutely nothing
that His mighty hand can't do
And He never is too busy
to help and comfort you.

GOD IS NEVER
BEYOND OUR REACH

No one ever sought the Father
And found He was not there,
And no burden is too heavy
To be lightened by a prayer,
No problem is too intricate
And no sorrow that we face
Is too deep and devastating
To be softened by His grace,
No trials and tribulations
Are beyond what we can bear
If we share them with Our Father
As we talk to Him in prayer—
And men of every color,
Every race and every creed
Have but to seek the Father
In their deepest hour of need—
God asks for no credentials,
He accepts us with our flaws,
He is kind and understanding
And He welcomes us because
We are His erring children
And He loves us everyone,
And He freely and completely
Forgives all that we have done,
Asking only if we're ready
To follow where He leads—
Content that in His wisdom
He will answer all our needs.

IN HOURS OF DISCOURAGEMENT
GOD IS OUR ENCOURAGEMENT

Sometimes we feel uncertain
And unsure of everything,
Afraid to make decisions,
Dreading what the day will bring—
We keep wishing it were possible
To dispel all fear and doubt
And to understand more readily
Just what life is all about—
God has given us the answers
Which too often go unheeded,
But if we search His promises
We'll find everything that's needed
To lift our faltering spirits
And renew our courage, too,
For there's absolutely nothing
Too much for God to do—
For the Lord is our salvation
And our strength in every fight,
Our redeemer and protector,
Our eternal guiding light—
He has promised to sustain us,
He's our refuge from all harms,
And underneath this refuge
Are the everlasting arms—
So cast your burden on Him,
Seek His counsel when distressed,
And go to Him for comfort
When you're lonely and oppressed—
For God is our encouragement
In trouble and in trials,

And in suffering and in sorrow
He will turn our tears to smiles.

YOU HELPED US BEFORE,
GOD, HELP US AGAIN

"O God, our help in ages past,
Our Hope in years to be"—
Look down upon this present
And see our need of Thee. . .
For in this age of unrest,
With danger all around,
We need Thy hand to lead us
To higher, safer ground. . .
We need Thy help and counsel
To make us more aware
That our safety and security
Lie solely in Thy care. . .
Give us strength and courage
To be honorable and true
Practicing Your precepts
In everything we do,
And keep us gently humble
In the greatness of Thy love
So someday we are fit to dwell
With Thee in peace above.

DayMaker
GREETING BOOKS

A Collection of Love Gifts
by Helen Steiner Rice

© 2002 by Barbour Publishing, Inc.
All poems © The Helen Steiner Rice Foundation. All rights reserved.

ISBN 1-58660-702-2

Cover images ©photonica
Book design by Kevin Keller| designconcepts

Published by Barbour Books, an imprint of Barbour Publishing, Inc.,
P.O. Box 719, Uhrichsville, Ohio 44683 www.barbourbooks.com

Printed in China.